DATE DUE		
00TB2019		

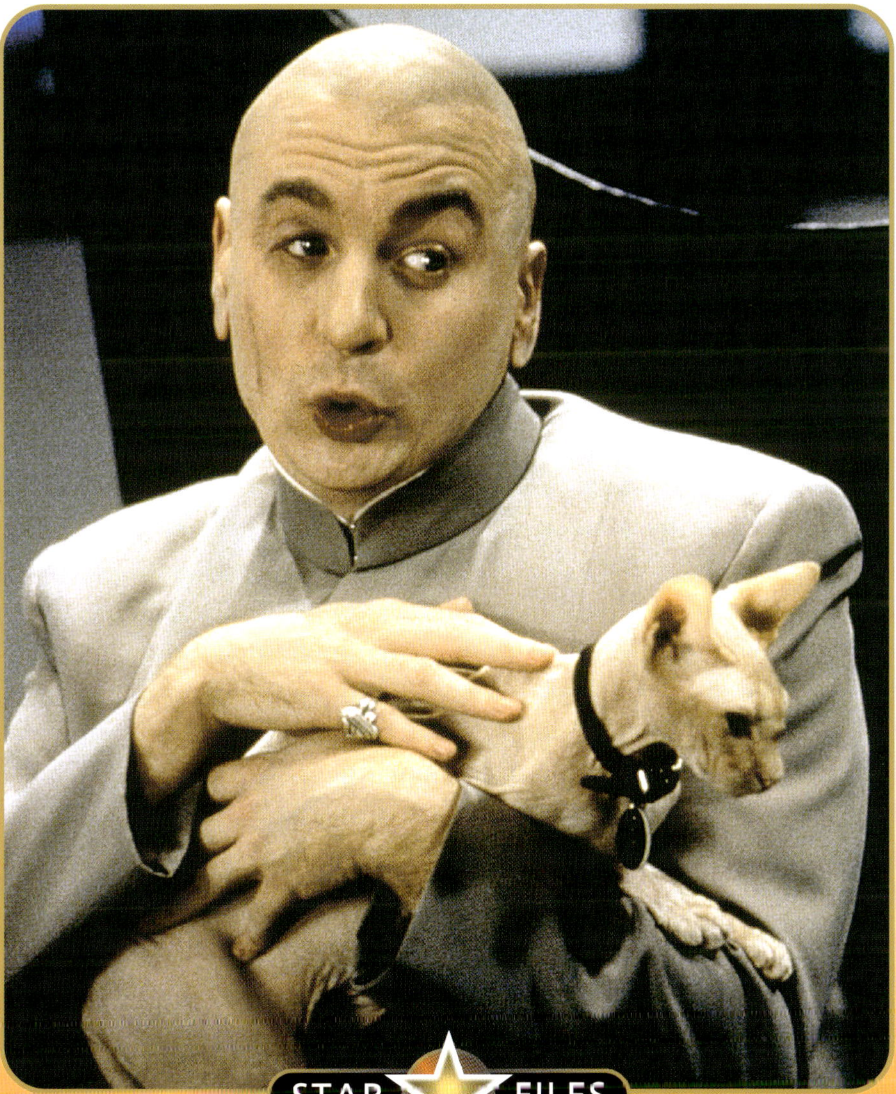

STAR FILES

Mike Myers

Paul Harrison

www.raintreepublishers.co.uk
Visit our website to find out more information about **Raintree** books.

To order:
 Phone 44 (0) 1865 888113
 Send a fax to 44 (0) 1865 314091
 Visit the Raintree Bookshop at **www.raintreepublishers.co.uk** to browse our catalogue and order online.

 Produced for Raintree by
White-Thomson Publishing Ltd
Bridgewater Business Centre
210 High Street, Lewes, BN7 2NH

First published in Great Britain by Raintree, Halley Court, Jordan Hill, Oxford OX2 8EJ, part of Harcourt Education.
Raintree is a registered trademark of Harcourt Education Ltd.

© Harcourt Education Ltd 2005
The moral right of the proprietor has been asserted.

All rights reserved. No part of this publication may be reproduced, stored in a retrieval system, or transmitted in any form or by any means, electronic, mechanical, photocopying, recording or otherwise, without either the prior written permission of the publishers or a licence permitting restricted copying in the United Kingdom issued by the Copyright Licensing Agency Ltd, 90 Tottenham Court Road, London W1T 4LP (www.cla.co.uk).

Editorial: Nick Hunter and Catherine Clarke
Design: Leishman Design and Michelle Lisseter
Picture Research: Nicola Hodgson
Production: Kevin Blackman
Project Management: Nicola Hodgson

Originated by Dot Gradations Ltd
Printed and bound in China by South China Printing Company

ISBN 1 844 43834 1
09 08 07 06 05
10 9 8 7 6 5 4 3 2 1

British Library Cataloguing in Publication Data
Harrison, Paul.
Mike Myers. – (Star Files)
791.4' 3' 028' 092
A full catalogue record for this book is available from the British Library.

Acknowledgements
The publishers would like to thank the following for permission to reproduce photographs: Allstar Picture Library pp. **4**, **19** (l), **19** (r), **20**, **21** (l), **21** (r), **22**, **23** (l), **25**, **27** (l), **27** (r), **28**, **29** (l), **35** (r), **37** (r), **38** (r), **40**, **41** (l); Corbis pp. **8** (r), **13** (l), **13** (r), **36**, **43** (l); Getty Images pp. **6** (l), **9**, **32**, **34** (r), **42**; Retna Pictures pp. **12**, **15** (l), **33** (r); Rex Features pp. **6** (r), **7**, **8** (l), **10**, **11** (l), **11** (r), **14**, **15** (r), **16** (l), **16** (r), **17** (l), **17** (r), **18** (l), **23** (r), **24**, **26**, **29** (r), **30**, **31** (l), **31** (r), **33** (l), **34** (l), **35** (l), **37** (l), **38** (l), **39**, **41** (r), **43** (r). Cover photograph reproduced with permission of Starmax Inc.

Quote sources: pp. **4**, **10**, **14**, **36**, **42** Entertainers with Byron Allen, Entertainmentstudios.com; pp. **12**, **18**, **19**, **24** *Wayne's World* DVD; pp. **12** *Mike Myers* by Lonnie Hull DuPont; p. **22**, **23**, **24** *Austin Powers in Goldmember* DVD; p. **24** *Austin Powers: The Spy Who Shagged Me* DVD; p. **25** Liese Spencer *Sight and Sound*; p. **25** Tom Long *The Detroit News*; p. **26** Interview at *Austin Powers in Goldmember* premiere; p. **41** Internet Movie Database.

The publishers would like to thank Voirrey Carr and Simone Apel for their assistance in the preparation of this book.

Every effort has been made to contact the copyright holders of any material reproduced in this book. Any omissions will be rectified in subsequent printings if notice is given to the publishers.

The paper used to print this book comes from sustainable resources.

Disclaimer: This book is not authorized or approved by Mike Myers.

Contents

Suburbs superstar	4
Starting out	8
Highs and lows	18
Yeah baby yeah	26
Behind the scenes	32
A monster hit	38
The Cat in the Hat	40
Future plans	42
Find out more	44
Glossary	46
Index	48

Any words appearing in the text in bold, **like this**, are explained in the Glossary. You can also look out for them in the Star words box at the bottom of each page.

Suburbs superstar

Mike Myers was a short, shy, geeky child from a quiet city in Canada who dreamed of being a comedian. He is now one of the most popular actors, writers and comedians of his day.

One of Mike's most famous characters is Austin Powers.

Old and new

In many ways, Mike is like an old-fashioned **variety show** star. He can sing, he can dance, he can act and he is very funny. Mike combines all these elements and makes them feel fresh and modern. Mike is a very physical performer. He loves **slapstick** humour. Slapstick is one of the most basic forms of humour.

ALL ABOUT MIKE

Full name: Michael Myers
Born: 25 May 1963
Place of birth: Scarborough, Ontario
Family: Father Eric; mother Alice; brothers Peter and Paul
Height: 5' 7" (1.7 metres)
Hobbies: Ice hockey and music
Married: Robin Ruzan (1993)
Big break: Joining the television programme *Saturday Night Live* in 1988
First major film: *Wayne's World*
Other interests: Has pet dogs and plays in a band

Star words

variety show mixture of songs, dances and comedy
slapstick people falling over or being hit in a funny way

Mike in a typical pose.

Mike is also a master of making up comedy as he goes along. This is called **improvising**.

Hard-working genius

Mike is difficult to classify. What is clear is that he is a comedy star. So how did Mike go from **suburbs** to superstar? The answer is simple. It took a bit of luck, a lot of hard work, and a large slice of genius.

❝ What I'd like to do is something extraordinary. ❞

Find out later

What is Mike's favourite sport?

Which character did Mike play in his first major film?

What films **inspired** Austin Powers?

improvise make things up as you go along
suburbs outskirts of a town or city where people live

Toronto lies by the side of Lake Ontario.

Simple childhood

Much of Mike's childhood was spent playing with his brothers in the basement of his house. As he got older, Mike became a typical suburban teenager. He took trips into town with his friends. They ate burgers and doughnuts and listened to music.

Home town boy

Mike grew up in Scarborough, Canada. This is a **suburb** of Toronto, which is a very large city. Scarborough was not a glamorous place. It just had the usual shopping centres, burger bars and doughnut shops. Later, Mike used this ordinary place as the **inspiration** for some of his work.

Leaving Liverpool

Mike's parents moved to Canada from Liverpool, England, in 1956. At that time people were being encouraged to **emigrate** from the UK to Canada. There they could start a new life in Canada's relatively empty cities.

Mike was awarded a star on the Hollywood Walk of Fame in 2002. His mother Alice and wife Robin went with him to the ceremony.

Star words   emigrate to leave one country and move to another

The Beatles were the world's favourite band when Mike was a child.

Number three

Mike's family was very close. Mike was the youngest of three boys. He was often picked on by his older brothers, Peter and Paul. Mike's parents even believed that Peter and Paul were funnier than Mike. Nevertheless, Mike's mother spotted his ability to entertain people. She did not want Mike to be just the family clown, however. She encouraged him to take dancing lessons from an early age.

Star fact

Mike got lots of helpful hints and tips from his mother, Alice. She had trained as an actress and she could also dance.

Beatlemania

The Beatles were from Liverpool, like Mike's parents. They were also the only people Mike knew of who sounded like his mum and dad. Mike thought he must be related to The Beatles!

Starting out

Drew Barrymore was one of the stars of the film *E.T. The Extra-Terrestrial*.

Mike's dancing lessons led to him being invited to **audition** for television adverts. When he was eight he danced in an advert for a car company. Mike also made adverts for famous soft drinks and **confectionary** companies. He made guest appearances on television programmes, too.

Friends on set

When Mike was nine, he appeared in an advert for an electricity company. An actress called Gilda Radner played Mike's mother in the advert. Mike and Gilda got on really well on **set**. Mike's brothers used to tease him about this.

Gilda Radner (centre, wearing sunglasses) with other members of the *Saturday Night Live* cast.

Child stars

Many top film stars worked on television programmes or films when they were children. The list includes Jodie Foster, Christina Ricci and Drew Barrymore.

Star words   **audition** interview for an actor or musician, where they show their skills

They said that Gilda was his 'girlfriend'. At that time neither Mike nor Gilda was famous, but Gilda later became a major comedy star.

Saturday Night Live

One night Mike was watching television with his family. A show came on called *Saturday Night Live*. It was a new type of comedy programme. It had lots of funny sketches and characters. It went on to become one of the most successful US comedy series ever. Mike recognized one of the stars of *Saturday Night Live* – it was Gilda Radner. Mike told his family that he would be on the programme one day, too. They thought Mike was being silly. How wrong they were.

Not so special

In 1977, when Mike was fourteen, he appeared in his first film. This was a short children's film called *Range Rider and the Calgary Kid*. The film was like an old-fashioned Western. Unfortunately, the film was not a success. This experience did not put Mike off performing, though. He was not going to give up. Bigger breaks were just around the corner.

Gilda Radner was awarded a Hollywood Walk of Fame star in 2003. That was fourteen years after she died.

Comedy and tragedy

Gilda Radner was a popular comic actress. She made her name with the comedy **troupe** Second City. Then she starred on *Saturday Night Live* and had her own one-woman show. She won an **Emmy Award** in 1978. Sadly, Gilda died of cancer in 1989. She was just 42.

confectionary sweets and chocolate
troupe group of performers

Mike worked hard at school. English and history were two of his favourite subjects. He was well known for missing early lessons because he was still in bed. Mike was not lazy, though. Around this time, Mike went to workshops at Second City. This was a famous comedy **troupe**. Second City was based in Chicago, USA, but also had a troupe in Toronto.

Dan Aykroyd was a star at both Second City and *Saturday Night Live*.

Stars of Second City

Many famous comedians worked at Second City, both in Chicago and Toronto. These include John Candy, Dan Aykroyd, Bill Murray and Eugene Levy.

A dilemma

As Mike was about to leave school in 1982, he applied to York University. He was accepted. On the day of his last High School exam he **auditioned** for a place with Second City. He was accepted there, too. Mike wondered what to do. Should he continue his education or try to become a comedian? His dream of being a comedian won. He decided to join Second City.

Second City

At Second City the comedians did not learn lines or rehearse routines. Instead, they **improvised** sketches on the spot. Mike proved to be an excellent improviser. He soon became one of Second City's star performers.

" Being adaptive is the most crucial lesson I've learnt. "

Star words adapt make changes because of differing circumstances

British comedian Neil Mullarkey was an early comic partner for Mike.

Adapt or die!
Mike was very good at improvised comedy. For this, you need to have a quick brain. There are no scripts. You never know what each person will say next. You have to be able to **adapt**. If you cannot adapt you will not be funny.

Mike has always been an energetic performer.

Bound for Britain
Mike was at Second City for a few years. Then he wanted to try something new. In 1985 he decided to try his luck in the UK, where his parents came from. Mike performed in small comedy clubs there. He also teamed up with a British comedian called Neil Mullarkey. Together they got a regular slot on a children's television programme called *The Wide Awake Club*. They even had their own series on UK television, called *Mullarkey and Myers*.

Wayne's World

Wayne Campbell is Mike's oldest comic character. 'I used to do the character at parties when I was about 11 or 12 through my **formative years**', says Mike. Wayne is like a typical North American teenager who loves rock music. The only difference is that Wayne made his own television programme in his parents' basement.

Back to Toronto

Mike spent some time in the UK, but then he started to get homesick. He returned to Toronto in 1986 and joined up with the Second City team again. While performing there he was spotted by some television **producers**. Mike was given the chance to be a television star on a new comedy show. The programme was called *It's Only Rock and Roll*. Each episode was a mix of music and comedy and lasted for half an hour.

> Wayne is sort of like everyone I grew up with.

An early picture of Mike as Wayne Campbell.

Star words formative years years that shape your character

Chicago is known as the Windy City.

Mike was one of the star performers. Audiences loved two of his characters in particular. These were a German television presenter called Dieter and a teenage heavy metal fan called Wayne Campbell. These characters would be important in Mike's later career.

The Windy City

It's Only Rock and Roll finished in 1987, when Mike was 24. Mike was then invited to work with the Second City **troupe** in Chicago. Chicago is also known as the Windy City. Coming from Canada, Mike was used to the icy winter weather. He loved being in Chicago.

A breath of fresh air

Second City Chicago was a very **prestigious** comedy troupe. It had a long and proud history. In recent years it had been in a slump. The show had become a bit stale. Mike helped to liven it up again. Mike did not stay with Second City for very long, though.

Waiting for inspiration

The character of Dieter was based on a German waiter Mike knew in Toronto. Dieter was weird, a bit scary and shouted at odd times. Mike has no idea whether the waiter ever saw Mike's Dieter character.

Mike as Dieter, looking typically serious.

prestigious having a good reputation

Award winner

Mike's comedy partner Dana Carvey is most famous in the USA for his work on *Saturday Night Live*. Dana first appeared on the show in 1986. He won an **Emmy** in 1993 for his comedy performances.

Dana Carvey was a star on *Saturday Night Live* even before Mike arrived.

In late 1988 Mike took a week off from Second City in Chicago. He went back to Canada to celebrate the fifteenth anniversary of Second City in Toronto. Mike did a comedy performance at the party. The guests found it very funny. A man called Lorne Michaels heard about Mike. Lorne was in charge of the famous US television comedy programme *Saturday Night Live*. Lorne decided to see Mike for himself.

A dream come true

Lorne met Mike and was very impressed. He offered Mike a job with *Saturday Night Live* as a writer and performer. This was a dream come true. Mike had told his family that he would be on the programme years earlier. Now he was on his way to New York to be a star.

Shy boy

Working on *Saturday Night Live* was a **daunting** experience for Mike. He knew all of the cast members, because he had seen them on television. Mike was an unknown, so he was a little shy and nervous for the first few weeks.

I always wanted to be on Saturday Night Live.

Here's Wayne

Things changed four weeks after Mike started. He introduced one of his favourite old characters, Wayne Campbell. Audiences loved Wayne.

Star words

daunting when a task seems quite scary

> **Star fact**
>
> Mike worked on *Saturday Night Live* for six years between 1989 and 1995. He received an Emmy Award for his writing on the programme in 1989.

Mike proved to the *Saturday Night Live* veterans that he had what it took. Mike got a regular slot for Wayne each week.

Dynamic duo

Wayne had a sidekick called Garth Algar. Garth was played by the comedian Dana Carvey. Mike and Dana worked very well together on screen. They would go on to have more success with their two teenage characters.

Dana Carvey, Lorne Michaels and Mike.

Eddie Murphy on *Saturday Night Live*.

Saturday stars

Lots of famous comedians have worked on *Saturday Night Live*, including Chevy Chase, James Belushi, Eddie Murphy, Adam Sandler and Will Ferrell.

veteran person with a lot of experience in something

Modest star

Despite the many fans that Mike has won, he does not take his success for granted. He says: 'I still believe that at any time the no-talent police will come and arrest me.'

Mike has millions of fans around the world. He also has a large number of celebrity fans. When Mike was on *Saturday Night Live* he got celebrities to appear with him. Lots of people wanted to be one of Mike's guests on the programme. These included Aerosmith, Mick Jagger, Danny DeVito, Wayne Gretzky, Bruce Willis, Tom Hanks and John Goodman.

Film star Bruce Willis was one of Mike's famous guests.

Rock legends Aerosmith were among the famous stars who appeared with Mike on *Saturday Night Live*.

Surprise guest

Usually Mike knew who would be appearing on the show, but one night he got a surprise. He was playing one of his most popular characters, Linda Richman.

Mike knew he already had Madonna and Roseanne Barr on the show. They were great guests, so he was not expecting anyone else.

Struck dumb

During the sketch Linda was talking about her favourite star, the famous singer Barbra Streisand. Then, in the middle of the sketch, who should walk past in the background? Streisand herself. Mike was stunned and speechless. The motor-mouth quick-witted comedian was lost for words. It made great television.

Madonna in disguise on *Saturday Night Live*.

On tour

Singing star Barbra Streisand (above) loved the character of Linda Richman. She thought Linda was so funny that she invited Mike to join her on tour. She wanted him to play Linda as a warm-up for the crowd. Mike was thrilled to accept.

Highs and lows

Wayne's World **co-star** Rob Lowe is a close friend of Mike's.

The plot
Wayne and Garth have their own television series called *Wayne's World*. It is very popular with teenagers. An evil executive, played by Rob Lowe, tries to take over *Wayne's World*. He nearly succeeds, but the boys win out in the end.

Wayne's World
Wayne was a great success on *Saturday Night Live*. Then Mike wanted to try to make a film of his favourite character. This would be Mike's first major film. It was a big gamble. Turning a short television sketch into a film is very difficult. Mike would not just be acting in the film either. He would be co-writing the film as well. This was a lot of work.

Deadline
Mike was faced with another problem, too. The filming had to be completed during the summer break of *Saturday Night Live*. This meant the film had to be made in just 34 days. This is a very short amount of time to make a film. If Mike felt nervous about his task, he did not show it. He was used to writing and **broadcasting** episodes of *Saturday Night Live* in a week. So, 34 days sounded like a long time.

Worried man
Mike did not feel so calm when shooting was finished. He saw an early print of the film and was convinced it would be a flop. He said: 'I couldn't stand it. I couldn't watch it. I thought it was awful. I was **inconsolable**.' Luckily, Mike was wrong about the film.

Star words   broadcast transmit by radio or television

Smash hit

Wayne's World was the surprise hit of 1992. Audiences loved the silliness of the film and loved the characters of Wayne and Garth. The film was even popular in countries that had never seen *Saturday Night Live*.

> "Wayne and Garth make everything fun. (Dana Carvey)"

Wayne loves hockey, just like Mike.

Wayne and Garth in action.

Waynespeak

Wayne's favourite sayings:
'party on'
'excellent!'
'we're not worthy'
'schwing!'

inconsolable unable to be cheered up

Dual parts

Mike had two parts in *So I Married an Axe Murderer*. He played the lead character, Charlie Mackenzie, and his father. Mike based the father on his own dad, Eric.

Mike as Charlie Mackenzie in *So I Married an Axe Murderer*.

Mike's next film, called *So I Married an Axe Murderer*, did not enjoy the same success as *Wayne's World*. Mike played the lead character in this comedy film. The script had been written and rewritten a few times before Mike read it. He thought that it could be funnier, so decided to rewrite it himself. Sometimes he was still writing a scene on the day that it was being filmed.

A flop

So I Married an Axe Murderer has lots of fans. Not enough people went to see it at the cinema for it to be a **commercial success**, though. Compared to the success of *Wayne's World*, it looked like a flop. It was a different kind of film and story from *Wayne's World*.

Pressure

In Hollywood, if one film is a success, there is a lot of pressure to make a **sequel**. *Wayne's World* was a big hit and people expected there to be a sequel. Sequels are sometimes not as good as the original films, however. This turned out to be the case with *Wayne's World 2*.

★ Star fact

Mike rewrote the script for *So I Married an Axe Murderer* with his old comedy partner, Neil Mullarkey.

Star words

commercial success something that sells well and makes a good profit

Mike and his *Axe Murderer* **co-star** Nancy Travis.

Good points
Wayne's World 2 was not a big success, but it still has many fans. Like *Wayne's World* the film pokes fun at other television programmes and films. Then there are the special **catchphrases** and guest appearances.

Success… not!
Wayne's World 2 was not as successful as the first film. The ideas were fun and fresh the first time around, but seemed stale the second time. Also, the whole idea for the film had to be changed just weeks before filming began because of legal reasons.

Take a break
It was hard for Mike when his films were not successful. Mike's friends advised him to take a proper break. Mike left *Saturday Night Live* and did not take on any new films for a while.

A hilarious scene from *Wayne's World 2*.

sequel follow up
catchphrase saying that is linked with a certain character

Laughs from the past

Mike still loves the old comedy programmes that his dad introduced him to. 'I am a huge Peter Sellers fan', he says. Sellers was in *The Goons*. He also made films including the popular *Pink Panther* series.

Peter Sellers as his most famous character, Inspector Clouseau.

Mike and his dad

Mike experienced personal sadness at this time, too. Mike's father Eric died just before *Wayne's World* became a huge success. He never saw Mike's great triumph.

Mike came from a very close family. He loved and trusted his parents. 'I used to tell him everything', said Mike of his father. The fact he was no longer there to share things with was very painful for Mike.

Happy household

Eric had a big influence on Mike. He taught Mike and his brothers that humour was a great cure for the troubles of life. Eric loved to laugh. He was always making jokes. It was no surprise that one of his sons grew up to be a comedian.

Late-night listening

Eric Myers introduced Mike and his brothers to the best of British comedy. The Myers family loved to listen to classic radio shows such as *The Goons*, or watch the television programme *Monty Python's Flying Circus*. These programmes were zany, lively and **chaotic**.

Star fact

Mike's dad taught him **cockney** rhyming slang. This is a way of talking where a word is replaced by another word or words that rhyme with it. So, instead of saying 'stairs' you say 'apples and pears'. Instead of saying 'telephone' you say 'dog and bone'.

Star words

cockney people from East London are called cockneys

The shows **inspired** many later comedians. They were also some of Eric's favourite programmes. They provided a great comic education for Mike, too.

> Some of the Monty Python cast in the film *Monty Python and the Holy Grail*.

Back to England

Eric wanted his ashes to be taken back to Liverpool, England, when he died. Eric always thought of Liverpool as his real home. Mike's family scattered Eric's ashes on the River Mersey (above). Mike said he thought that this was the best thing he had ever done.

chaotic confused and lacking order

Mike has always worked very hard. He is also famous for **improvising** during filming. Mike calls this making it 'funnier than written'. However, he still wants his scripts to be as funny as possible.

Late nights

Mike often worked late into the night when he was writing his material. This was especially true when he was working on *Saturday Night Live*. The writers would meet on a Tuesday to discuss ideas. They then had to get material ready by Friday for **rehearsal**. There was very little time to put each programme together. Even the quickest writers were pushed for time. Sometimes Mike ended up sleeping in the building.

Mike often worries about his work.

Worried writer

Often Mike will do draft after draft of his work. He is never sure if it is good enough. 'I sit and I worry and I rewrite madly', says Mike.

Star fact

When Mike first worked on *Saturday Night Live* as a writer he did not have an office, or even a desk to work at. It is said that he sat on the floor by the elevators to write his material. Mike worked his way up to having a desk. Eventually he got his own office.

Rocket fuel

Mike is very serious about his work. Dana Carvey thinks that Mike's drive was really important when making *Wayne's World*. 'Mike's obsession for detail and work ethic really was the rocket **propellant** for the movie', he says.

" The only thing I hate about movies is getting up early. "

Star words   rehearsal practice

Mike as club owner Steve Rubell in *54*.

Acting up

When Mike does something, he likes to do it well. It was no surprise then that when he tried serious acting he was very good at it. His first attempt was in 1998 in a film called *54*. It was hard to believe that it really was Mike playing the character of Steve Rubell. He was the owner of the nightclub Studio 54. Audiences were not used to seeing Mike play straight roles. Also, he had a wig and a false nose and looked very different.

New character

Before taking on the part in *54* Mike had taken his friends' advice to have a break. For a while Mike did no writing or performing. It is very difficult for a hard worker like Mike to stop thinking about work, though. He was soon trying to decide what he would do next. By 1997 he was back with a new character. Mike was about to hit the big time again.

Winning performance

The film *54* was not a success, but Mike got good reviews for his performance. One critic said: 'Mike Myers' Rubell is the best thing about the movie'. Another said: 'Myers is wonderful as nightclub owner Steve Rubell…'

propellant fuel

Yeah baby yeah

Famous friends

In the first Austin Powers film Mike plays both Austin and Dr Evil. Mike also wrote the film and was one of the **producers**. Another of the film's producers was Hollywood star Demi Moore.

In 1997 Mike was back with a new character and a new film, *Austin Powers: International Man of Mystery*. Mike did not know if people would like it. After all, his last two films had been disappointing. He should not have worried. The film was the comedy hit of the year.

Old inspiration

Austin Powers was **inspired** by some of Mike's favourite films from the 1960s. The biggest influences were the James Bond films and other spy films. In the film, Mike plays 1960s British secret agent Austin Powers. Austin was frozen in the 1960s so he can return in the 1990s. He does battle with his rival, the **villain** Dr Evil. Both Austin and Dr Evil have problems adjusting to life in the 1990s. This leads to some very amusing situations. The film was fun for Mike to make, as well. He said that Dr Evil was his favourite character in the film because he 'always wanted to play a bad guy'.

Back on top

Austin Powers: International Man of Mystery really caught the public's imagination. They loved the characters and the new **catchphrases** such as 'Yeah, baby!' and 'Oh, behave'. Mike was a star again.

Demi Moore helped Mike to bring *Austin Powers* to the screen.

Star words villain character who is bad

⭐ Star fact

During a **test-screen** of *Austin Powers*, the film actually broke. Mike rushed to the front of the cinema. He entertained the audience until the film could be repaired. The audience loved it!

Dr Evil is one of Mike's greatest characters.

Copy cat

Mike copied some of the most famous Bond villains. Dr Evil is based on the cat-loving Ernst Blofeld, who appears in several of the Bond films. Both of these characters are bald and speak with an odd accent. The character Random Task is a send-up of Bond baddie Odd Job in *Goldfinger*.

Mike with **co-star** Elizabeth Hurley.

test-screen early preview of a film

Legal problems

Not everyone is a fan of the Austin Powers films. The people who make the James Bond films wanted Mike to change the name of *Austin Powers in Goldmember*. They thought the name was too close to the Bond film, *Goldfinger*. Mike was eventually allowed to use the title, though.

The success continues

The first Austin Powers film was a great success. This meant that people expected **sequels**. Despite the bad experience of *Wayne's World 2*, Mike wanted to try it. In fact, Mike made two more Austin Powers films.

Lost mojo

The first sequel was called *Austin Powers: The Spy Who Shagged Me*. In this film Austin has his life force, or mojo, stolen. Powers has to travel back in time to stop the theft from happening. He is helped by Felicity Shagwell, played by Heather Graham. The film features the first appearance of Mini Me, the tiny Dr Evil lookalike.

New villain

The third film was called *Austin Powers in Goldmember*. In that film Dr Evil returns with another scheme to take over the world. He plans to travel back in time and kidnap Austin's father, Nigel Powers. Nigel is played by Michael Caine. Austin must travel back in time again to stop Dr Evil and a new **villain** called Goldmember. Again, Mike plays Dr Evil. He also plays Goldmember.

Dr Evil and Mini Me. Mini Me was played by actor Verne Troyer.

Mike and co-star Heather Graham.

The A-list
Lots of great stars have appeared in the Austin Powers films. Among the famous names are: Gwyneth Paltrow, Tom Cruise, John Travolta and Britney Spears. Popular singer Beyoncé Knowles played Austin's sidekick, Foxxy Cleopatra, in *Goldmember*.

Room to grow
The clever thing about these films is that the characters develop and change. New characters are introduced, such as Mini Me. Old characters are given new life. They are shown earlier in time with younger actors playing them. These changes helped to make the films a success. The new Austin Powers films still seemed fresh. The range and number of jokes was much greater. There was no danger of these films failing in the way that *Wayne's World 2* had done.

Beyoncé Knowles and Michael Caine at the US premiere of *Austin Powers in Goldmember*.

Cool cars

It is not just what Austin Powers looked like that helped explain his character. His cars were just as important. What else would Austin Powers drive around in but a Jaguar painted with a Union Jack? When Austin travels back in time in *Austin Powers: The Spy Who Shagged Me*, what kind of car does he make the journey in? The Volkswagen Beetle – a classic symbol of the 1960s and the 1990s.

Mike style

Mike has brought a whole range of different characters to life. Andrew Adamson is a **director** who has worked with Mike. He says: 'The thing with Mike is that he's somebody who can really create a character.' An important part of creating a character is the clothes they wear. Mike loves dressing up.

Distinctive

Each of Mike's characters has had a very distinctive look. Sometimes the clothes are quite realistic. At other times the clothes are really bizarre.

Realistic

Wayne Campbell is a heavy metal-loving teenager. His ripped jeans and t-shirt are like a uniform. The clothes Mike wore when playing Steve Rubell in *54* are typical of the 1970s, when the film was set.

Beyoncé poses next to Austin's car, the Shaguar.

Star words

director person in charge of making a film
prosthetics false attachments such as a nose or ears

Some of the outrageous costumes from *Austin Powers in Goldmember*.

Cartoon capers

In real life, no one really wore clothes exactly like Austin Powers. What he wears is an over-the-top idea of 1960s' fashion. This adds to the **cartoonish** fun of the character. Fans of the films love these fun clothes. Some of them even dress up like characters in the films!

Outrageous

In contrast, the clothes of Austin Powers are out of this world. He wears big velvet suits, frilly shirts and Cuban-heeled boots. Who could forget Austin's Union Jack underpants? All of these clothes match Austin's over-the-top personality.

When you are as popular as Mike, fans come by the bus-load to see you.

Stick-on bits

Of course, it is not just clothes that make up a character's appearance. Just look at the range of hairstyles Mike has worn on **set**. Mike also uses false teeth and **prosthetics**, like the false nose he wore as Steve Rubell in *54*.

cartoonish like something out of a cartoon

Behind the scenes

Out of the limelight

Mike is very shy. He tries to keep his life as private as possible. An example of this is his pet dogs. Mike has three dogs, but no one seems sure what they are called. One story says they are named after ice hockey players. Another story says he keeps the names secret so the dogs do not get kidnapped.

During the time Mike was working in Chicago, in 1987, he enjoyed going to watch ice hockey. One match he went to was between the Chicago Blackhawks and his local team from Canada, the Toronto Maple Leafs.

Lucky meeting

During the game Mike caught the **puck** when it was accidentally hit into the crowd. Anyone who catches a puck can keep it, so Mike had a fantastic **memento** from the game. Watching the same game was an actress and **scriptwriter** called Robin Ruzan. The story goes that Robin also caught a puck that night – on the head! Mike went to help her. They hit it off and started dating. The couple got married in 1993.

Mike's favourite team, the Toronto Maple Leafs.

Star words

puck small, thick rubber disc used in ice hockey
memento object kept as a reminder or souvenir

Helping hand

Robin has played her part in the success of the Austin Powers films. She helped Mike write some parts of the films, most notably the 'Just the two of us' scene in *Austin Powers: The Spy Who Shagged Me*. Dr Evil and Mini Me do their own version of this song.

Family joke to TV hit

Robin was not the only member of the Ruzan family to help Mike. He based his popular *Saturday Night Live* character Linda Richman on Robin's mother, Linda. Mike used to **impersonate** Linda as a joke for friends and family. Eventually he tried the character out on *Saturday Night Live*. She was a great success.

Robin, Mike and Robin's mother, Linda. Linda **inspired** one of Mike's comic characters.

Mike with his wife Robin.

Talk show queen

Linda Richman is the host of a chat show called *Coffee Talk*. Like most of Mike's characters she has her own **catchphrases**. Linda's most famous one was 'I'm verklempt'. This is a **Yiddish** expression. It means 'I am overcome' or 'upset'.

scriptwriter someone who writes scripts for films, television programmes or adverts

Great Gretzky

While Mike was playing Wayne on *Saturday Night Live* in 1989, he had the chance to play hockey against Wayne Gretzky. He was so good at hockey that he was known as 'The Great One'. He retired in 1999.

Ice hockey legend Wayne Gretzky.

Mike works so hard he does not get a lot of free time. When he gets spare time he uses it on his two great passions: ice hockey and rock music.

Favourite team

The Toronto Maple Leafs is Mike's favourite hockey team. He watches them whenever he can. The Toronto Maple Leafs formed in the 1920s. Their **glory days** were in the 1940s and 1960s when they won the Stanley Cup many times. This is the prize awarded to the champions of the US National Hockey League. The last time they won the cup was in 1967. Mike has had a long wait to see further Stanley Cup success.

Ice hockey is the fastest team game in the world. It takes real skill to skate quickly.

Dedicated

Mike likes playing ice hockey, too. When he was taking a break from films before writing the first Austin Powers film, he tried to improve his game. He learnt how to be a better skater so he could be a better player. That takes **dedication**.

Tea time

Mike also loves music and even plays in a band. The group is called Ming Tea and also includes Susanna Hoffs. She was the lead singer and guitarist with the famous girl group The Bangles.

Star words glory days successful times

Ming Tea has released two singles. They were called 'BBC' and 'Daddy wasn't there'. Both songs featured in Austin Powers films. Ming Tea played some of the music in the Austin Powers films. They also feature in small breaks in the filming. The band was invited to be the house band at Johnny Depp's nightclub, The Viper Rooms, in Los Angeles.

Folk lover

Mike does not just love rock music. One of his favourite performers is folk singer Joni Mitchell. She is also a fellow Canadian.

Jay Roach on **set** with Mike as Austin Powers.

Austin Powers with Ming Tea.

Friends in high places

Jay Roach is a friend of Mike's and a big hockey fan, too. He was the **director** of the Austin Powers films. After making *Austin Powers: International Man of Mystery* he went on to make a film about ice hockey called *Mystery, Alaska*. Guess who had a small role in the film? Ice hockey fan and friend Mike Myers!

dedication working hard at something

Late-night worker

Mike does not like getting up early. He prefers to work through the night, going to bed in the early hours. He then has a long lie in before starting to work again. 'I like to write fast', says Mike. That is just as well, or he would never get to bed!

Mike often works for most of the night.

Difficult to work with?

No one doubts that Mike is a very hard-working professional. Not everyone agrees that Mike is an easy person to work with, though. When Mike was at Second City, he was not an ideal co-worker. Other comedians there remember that he did not want to be part of a team. No one could deny that Mike was very good at what he did, however.

Sprockets

No matter what people thought of Mike, no one expected him to end up with legal problems. This is what happened when Mike agreed to make a film about another one of his *Saturday Night Live* characters. It was about the character Dieter. Mike was going to write and star in it. The movie was going to be called *Sprockets*.

About turn

Mike soon hit a problem. No matter how many times he rewrote the script, he never thought it was funny enough. He took a hard decision. He pulled out of the film. The studio that was making the film was Universal. They were not happy with Mike's decision and decided to **sue** him. Mike then decided to sue Universal. He claimed that they had treated him badly. Neither Mike nor Universal would back down. Someone was needed to sort out the mess. That man was Jeffrey Katzenberg.

Star words   sue go to court to get money from someone

A deal

Katzenberg was one of the owners of another studio called DreamWorks SKG. The studio had links with Mike and Universal. A deal was reached. Universal would stop suing Mike if he made a different film for them. Both sides were happy with the deal. Universal would get a Mike Myers film. Mike would be free from legal battles to make new films.

Leonardo di Caprio starred in the DreamWorks film *Catch Me if You Can*.

Dream workers

DreamWorks SKG was set up by Steven Spielberg, Jeffrey Katzenberg and David Geffen in 1994. The studio has produced many hit films, such as *Catch Me if You Can* and *Antz*.

Mike with DreamWorks chief, Jeffrey Katzenberg.

A monster hit

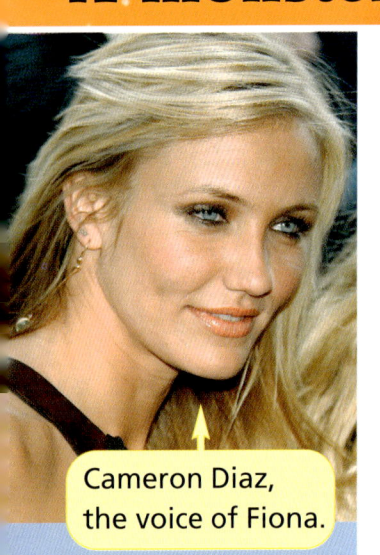

Cameron Diaz, the voice of Fiona.

The end of the legal dispute meant Mike could **promote** the film he had made for Jeffrey Katzenberg's DreamWorks studio. The film was called *Shrek*. The surprising thing was that Mike would not be seen on the film. It was an **animated film**. Katzenberg had hired Mike for his voice.

Monster man
Mike provided the voice for the film's main character, an ogre called Shrek. Mike was not the only star to work on the film. Other voices were provided by Cameron Diaz, Eddie Murphy and John Lithgow. Mike also provided the voice for one of the three blind mice in the film.

All change
When the film was finished everyone was very happy with the result. Well, nearly everyone.

The main characters from *Shrek*: Donkey, Shrek, Fiona and Farquaad.

The plot
Shrek is an ogre who wants to be left alone. The evil ruler Lord Farquaad has overrun Shrek's swamp with fairytale characters. Shrek agrees to rescue Fiona, the woman Farquaad wants to marry, from a dragon. In return, Farquaad agrees to remove the fairytale **'squatters'**. However, Fiona loves Shrek, not Farquaad, and she has a secret: she is really an ogre.

Star words

animated film film made using drawings, puppets or computer graphics instead of actors

> **Star fact**
>
> The character of Shrek was created by the famous children's author William Steig.

Mike was not happy. He did not feel that his voice for Shrek was funny enough. Mike was convinced that it would be funnier if the character had a Scottish accent. The **directors** of the film agreed.

Expensive

To change the recording at this stage would be very expensive. Surprisingly Jeffrey Katzenberg said it would be OK. Two weeks later the **voice-over** was recorded again and the film was ready. Jeffrey Katzenberg was right to let Mike re-record his lines. He knew the film was good and was sure it would be a success. It was. You could say the film was a monster hit!

Perfect combination

DreamWorks studios had had hits before with films like *Antz*. That film worked well because it mixed fantastic animation with top actors' voices. The script was funny and appealed to both adults and children. *Shrek* worked for exactly the same reasons. The animation was **cutting edge** and the jokes had audiences laughing. Mike had starred in another hit film.

Mike's highest earning films

Shrek: US#482.7 million

The Spy Who Shagged Me: US#310.9 million

Goldmember: US#296.6 million

Wayne's World: US#183.1 million

Austin Powers: US#67.7 million

Mike with a model of his character Shrek.

---

cutting edge newest way of doing something
voice-over voice given to a cartoon character

The Cat in the Hat

Who was Dr Seuss?

Dr Seuss wrote *The Cat in the Hat*. His real name was Theodor Seuss Geisel. He was born in 1904. He wrote more than 40 books for children. He wrote such classics as *Green Eggs and Ham*, *Too Many Daves*, and *The Cat in the Hat Comes Back*. Dr Seuss died in 1991.

Back in 2000, Jeffrey Katzenberg sorted out a legal problem between Mike and Universal Studios. As part of that deal Mike agreed to make a new film for Universal. In 2003 that film was released.

Hat-wearing hero

The film sees Mike playing a brand new character. This time the character was not one of Mike's own inventions. This one was a children's book classic. Mike was playing Dr Seuss' famous Cat in the Hat.

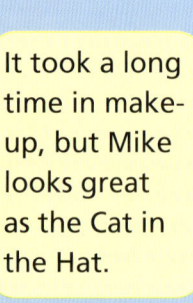

It took a long time in make-up, but Mike looks great as the Cat in the Hat.

Star words   anarchic no respect for rules

The Cat arrives in an amazing car.

Suffering for his film
Mike has always used make-up and costumes to create a character. He has never used it to the extent he does in *The Cat in the Hat*, though. The Cat costume was hot and uncomfortable. Even going to the toilet was difficult.

'To play the Cat is a great honour', says Mike.

What a mess
The book *The Cat in the Hat* tells of a magical, **anarchic** cat who wears a big, stripy top hat. When two children sit watching the rain on a cold, wet day, the cat turns up. He tries to entertain the children with games. Instead, he brings chaos to the house.

Madcap Mike
The story is funny and silly with lots of **madcap** humour. It is an ideal role for Mike, who loves the whole idea of being silly. Unlike *Shrek*, *The Cat in the Hat* is not animated. Instead it is live action. This means that Mike has to be turned into the character of the cat. To do this, Mike had to spend three hours each day in make-up.

★ Star fact
The *Cat in the Hat* is one of the best-selling children's books of all time.

Future plans

Home lover
Mike is very proud of being a Canadian. Mike says: 'Toronto is always home. There's a certain attitude there that doesn't exist anywhere else.'

Mike is happy to sign autographs for fans.

Mike has been very successful. Now he can afford to pick and choose what he does next. Perhaps he will invent another new character. Or he may take more acting roles like the one he played in *54* or the more recent film, *View From the Top*.

Animated return
Busy actors like Mike always have work to do. In 2004, *Shrek 2* was released. The film features Mike's **co-stars** from the first film, Cameron Diaz and Eddie Murphy. The plot for this film sees Shrek and Fiona travelling to the kingdom of Far, Far Away to visit Fiona's parents. They have lots of adventures on the way.

Star words SARS virus fast-spreading disease that can kill people

All the stars are back together again for *Shrek 2*.

Missing films

Mike had a guest role in *View From the Top* in 2003. He has also been in two other films called *McClintock's Peach* and *Pete's Meteor*. Both these films had good reviews at previews, but neither film has found a **distributor** yet.

View From the Top star Gwyneth Paltrow.

Austin Powers 4?

What many fans would like to know is whether there will be another Austin Powers film. Mike has been reported as saying that he is not keen, but there have been rumours that there may be another film.

Public support

Mike had not planned for the outbreak of the **SARS virus** in his beloved Toronto in 2003. Mike took time out of his busy schedule to reassure people that Toronto was still a safe place to visit. He even appeared on the popular US programme *The Tonight Show* to **promote** the city.

Extraordinary man

Mike is certainly a busy superstar, but at heart he is still a boy from the **suburbs** who loves his town and is proud of his country. When you look at what he has achieved he has certainly done 'something extraordinary', to quote his own words.

distributor company that supplies films to cinemas

Find out more

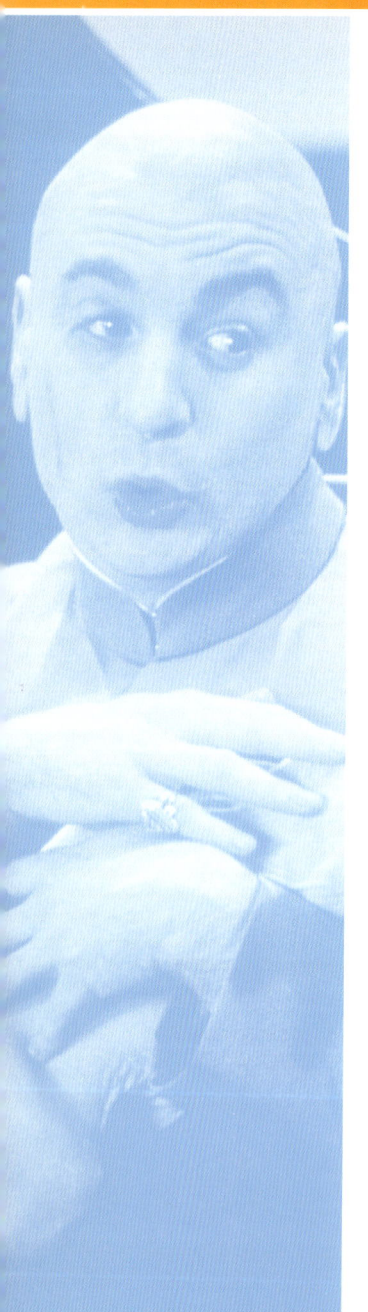

Books

Austin Powers: How to be an International Man of Mystery, Michael McCullers (G P Putnam's Sons, 1999)
Mike Myers, Lonnie Hull Dupont (Chelsea House Publishers, 2003)
Mike's World: The Life of Mike Myers, Martin Knelman (Firefly Books, 2003)
Shagadelically Speaking: The Words and the World of Austin Powers, Lance Gould (Warner, 1999)
Shrek: Essential Guide, Steven Spielberg, Jeffrey Katzenberg, David Geffen (Dorling Kindersley, 2004)
Wayne's World: Extreme Close-up, Mike Myers, Robin Ruzan (Hyperion Books, 1992)
The World of Austin Powers, Andy Lane (Universe Publishing, 2002)

Filmography

Shrek 2 (2004)
The Cat in the Hat (2003)
View From the Top (2003)
Austin Powers in Goldmember (2002)
Shrek (2001)
Mystery, Alaska (1999)
Austin Powers: The Spy Who Shagged Me (1999)
54 (1998)
Austin Powers: International Man of Mystery (1997)

Wayne's World 2 (1993)
So I Married an Axe Murderer (1993)
Wayne's World (1992)
Range Rider and the Calgary Kid (1977)

Television
Saturday Night Live (1989–1995)
It's Only Rock and Roll (1987)
The Wide Awake Club (1985)

Websites
For information on Austin Powers:
www.austinpowers.com
For information on *Shrek* and *Shrek 2*:
www.shrek.com
www.shrek2.com
For information on Dr Seuss:
www.seuss.org
www.seussville.com
For more information on ice hockey and the Toronto Maple Leafs:
www.nhl.com
www.torontomapleleafs.com
www.icehockeyuk.co.uk

Disclaimer
All the Internet addresses (URLs) given in this book were valid at the time of going to press. However, due to the dynamic nature of the Internet, some addresses may have changed, or sites may have ceased to exist since publication. While the author, packager and publishers regret any inconvenience this may cause readers, no responsibility for any such changes can be accepted by either the author, packager or the publishers.

Glossary

adapt make changes because of differing circumstances

anarchic no respect for rules

animated film film made using drawings, puppets or computer graphics instead of actors

audition interview for an actor or musician, where they show their skills

broadcast transmit by radio or television

cartoonish like something out of a cartoon

catchphrase saying that is linked with a certain character

chaotic confused and lacking order

cockney people from East London are called cockneys

co-stars actors appearing together in a film or television show

commercial success something that sells well and makes a good profit

confectionary sweets and chocolate

cutting edge newest way of doing something

daunting when a task seems quite scary

dedication working hard at something

director person in charge of making a film

distributor company that supplies films to cinemas

emigrate to leave one country and move to another

Emmy Award important US television award

formative years years that shape your character

glory days successful times

impersonate copy or imitate

improvise make things up as you go along

inconsolable unable to be cheered up

inspire give someone the idea or motivation to do something

madcap crazy

memento object kept as a reminder or souvenir

prestigious having a good reputation

producer person who organizes the people and the money to make a film or television show

promote tell people about a new product

propellant fuel

prosthetics false attachments such as a nose or ears

puck small, thick rubber disc used in ice hockey

rehearsal practice

SARS virus fast-spreading disease that can kill people

scriptwriter someone who writes scripts for films, television programmes or adverts

sequel follow up

set part of a film studio where a film or advert is shot

slapstick people falling over or being hit in a funny way

squatter someone who takes over your house and lives there when you do not want them to

suburbs outskirts of a town or city where people live

sue go to court to get money from someone

test-screen early preview of a film

troupe group of performers

variety show mixture of songs, dances and comedy

veteran person with a lot of experience in something

villain character who is bad

voice-over voice given to a cartoon character

Yiddish Jewish language or dialect

Index

Adamson, Andrew 30
Aerosmith 16
Aykroyd, Dan 10

Bangles, The 35
Barr, Roseanne 17
Barrymore, Drew 8
Beatles, The 7
Belushi, James 15

Caine, Michael 28
Candy, John 10
Caprio, Leonardo di 37
Carvey, Dana 14–15, 24
Chase, Chevy 15
Cruise, Tom 29

Depp, Johnny 35
DeVito, Danny 16
Diaz, Cameron 38, 42
DreamWorks 37–39

Ferrell, Will 15
Foster, Jodie 8

Geffen, David 37
Goodman, John 16
Graham, Heather 28, 29
Gretzky, Wayne 16, 34

Hanks, Tom 16
Hoffs, Susanna 35
Hurley, Elizabeth 27

Jagger, Mick 16

Katzenberg, Jeffrey 36–40
Knowles, Beyoncé 29–30

Levy, Eugene 10
Lithgow, John 38
Lowe, Rob 18

Madonna 17
Michaels, Lorne 14–15
Ming Tea 35
Mitchell, Joni 35
Moore, Demi 26
Mullarkey, Neil 11, 20
Murphy, Eddie 15, 38, 42
Murray, Bill 10
Myers, Eric 4, 22, 23
Myers, Mike
  auditions 8, 10
  awards 15
  books 44
  childhood 6–10
  films 25, 30–31, 42
    Austin Powers
      26–28, 35, 39
    The Cat in the Hat
      40–41
    Goldmember 28–29, 39
    McClintock's Peach 43
    Mystery, Alaska 35
    Pete's Meteor 43
    Range Rider and the
      Calgary Kid 9
    Shrek 38–39, 41
    Shrek 2 42–43
    So I Married an
      Axe Murderer 20
    Sprockets 36
    The Spy Who
      Shagged Me 28, 30,
      33, 39
    View From the Top 42
    Wayne's World 4, 12,
      18–22, 24, 39
    Wayne's World 2
      20–21, 28–29
  hobbies 34–35
  marriage 32–33
  parents 4, 6–7, 22–23

television
  It's Only Rock and
    Roll 12–13
  Mullarkey and
    Myers 11
  Saturday Night Live 4,
    8–9, 14–19, 21, 24,
    33–34
  The Tonight Show 43
  The Wide Awake
    Club 11
websites 45

Paltrow, Gwyneth 29, 43

Radner, Gilda 8–9
Ricci, Christina 8
Roach, Jay 35
Ruzan, Linda 33
Ruzan, Robin 32

Sandler, Adam 15
Second City 10–14, 36
Sellers, Peter 22
Seuss, Dr 40
Smith, Will 33
Spears, Britney 29
Spielberg, Steven 37
Steig, William 39
Streisand, Barbra 17

Travis, Nancy 21
Travolta, John 29

Universal Studios 36, 37, 40

Willis, Bruce 16

Titles in the *Star Files* series include:

Halle Berry
Liz Gogerly
Hardback   1 844 43829 5

Jennifer Lopez
Kay Barnham
Hardback   1 844 43830 9

Justin Timberlake
Dan Whitcombe
Hardback   1 844 43833 3

Mike Myers
Paul Harrison
Hardback   1 844 43834 1

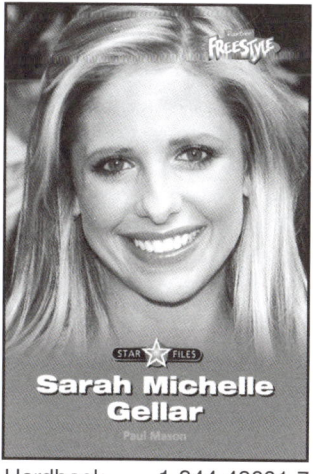

Sarah Michelle Gellar
Paul Mason
Hardback   1 844 43831 7

Will Smith
Mark Stewart
Hardback   1 844 43832 5

Find out about the other titles in this series on our website www.raintreepublishers.co.uk